Blueberry's Gift

Written by Tenney Mudge

Illustrated by Erika Cummings

A portion of the proceeds of this book will be donated to Hoofbeats Therapeutic Riding Center.

Copyright © 2019 by Tenney Mudge and Erika Cummings

All rights reserved, including the right of reproduction in whole or in part in any form without the express written permission of the publisher.

1 3 5 7 9 10 8 6 4 2

Library of Congress Control Number: 2019941843
Blueberry's Gift
by Tenney Mudge
illustrated by Erika Cummings

p. cm.
1. Juvenile Nonfiction: Animals—Horses
2. Juvenile Nonfiction: Disabilities & Special Needs
3. Juvenile Nonfiction: Sports & Recreation—Equestrian

I. Mudge, Tenney, 1958– II. Cummings, Erika, 1994– III. Title.
ISBN 13: 978-1-7339720-2-4 (softcover : alk. paper)

Harbour Books
An imprint of Mariner Publishing
A division of Mariner Media, Inc.
131 West 21st St.
Buena Vista, VA 24416
Tel: 540-264-0021
www.marinermedia.com

Printed in the United States of America

This book is printed on acid-free paper meeting the requirements of the American Standard for Permanence of Paper for Printed Library Materials.

One day a girl came to visit me. She lived in the mountains too.

She had brown hair that was long like my tail.

I was excited to learn that I had a gift!

I needed to work hard to be brave and strong, so I could make the world a better place.

So every time things got hard, I said, "I'm OK! I need to be brave and strong. I am going to make the world a better place."

The girl listened and smiled.

This time when I asked what I could do with my life I knew the answer!

I am a pony. I am brave and strong. I can help carry people!

I can help people be brave and strong,
so they can make the world a better place too.

The girl loved me most of all, and I loved her.

The girl and all the people cheered.
Together we walked, ran, danced, and smiled.

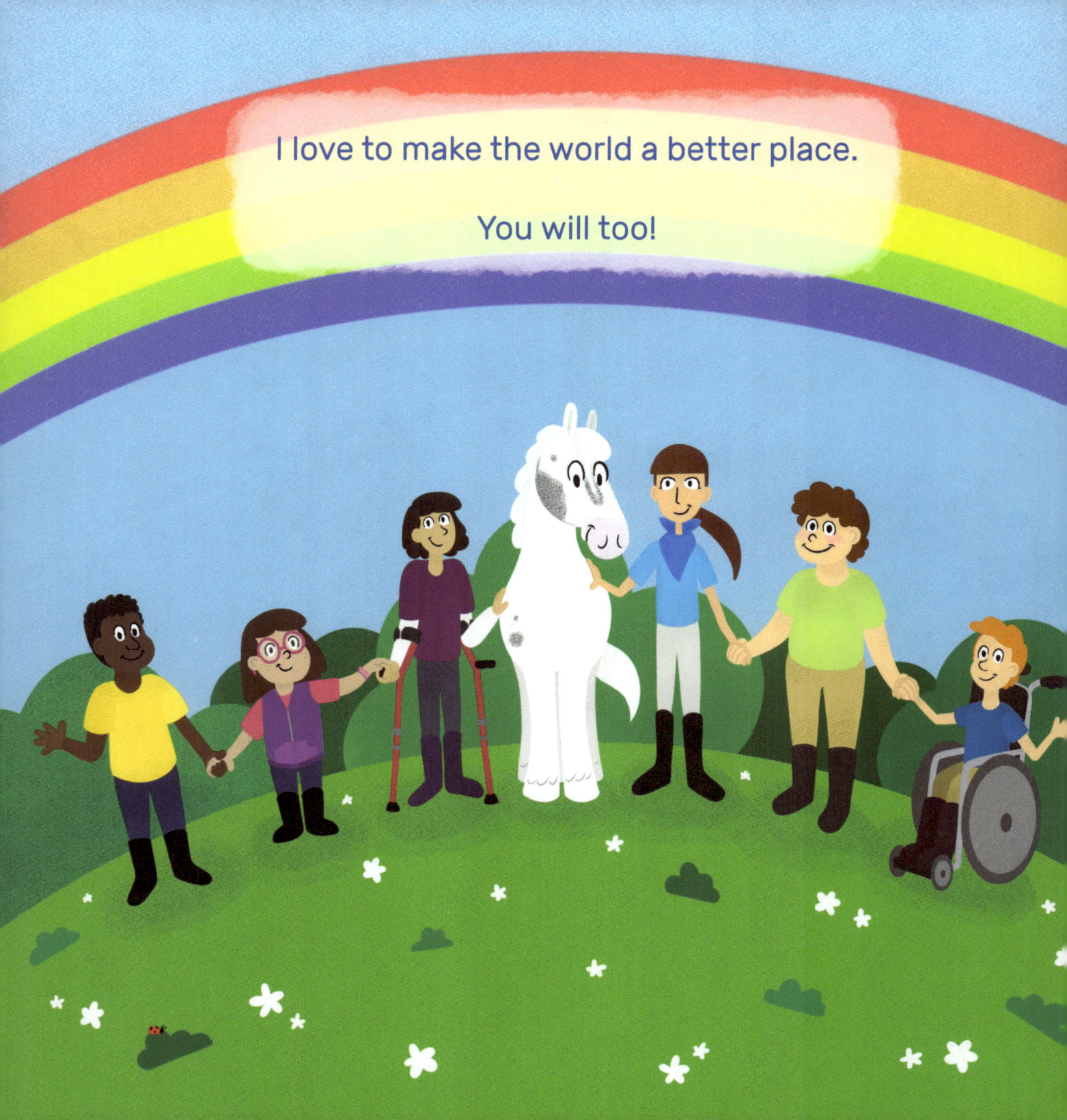

The Real Blueberry

Deepest love and honor to Blueberry and his legacy of inspiration, for Hoofbeats Therapeutic Riding Center, for all the therapy horses of the world, and for the people who help them share their gifts.

Meet the Author

Tenney Mudge partnered with Blueberry for 25 years. When Blueberry exhibited his calm strengths to serve children, she nurtured him on a path to become a nationally-acclaimed therapy horse at Hoofbeats Therapeutic Riding Center near her home in Lexington, Virginia. Tenney has been a longtime board member and volunteer at Hoofbeats serving as a horse handler, fundraiser, and event director.

A native of Northport, New York, and a graduate of Cornell University, Tenney worked as staff newsletter writer for the American Horse Protection Association in Washington, DC. When Tenney lost her dog in a collar accident, she invented and patented the KeepSafe® Break-Away Collar to prevent such a tragedy from happening to other dogs.

Meet the Illustrator

Erika Cummings is a local artist from Lexington, Virginia. As a kid, she always had a passion for two things: animals and drawing.

A graduate from Longwood University, she uses her drawing skills and knowledge at Mariner Media to illustrate children's books and make their characters and stories come to life. She illustrated *Ruby at the Gate* during her summer internship at Mariner Media in 2018.

Before she found work in illustration, she worked at a local animal shelter for several summers caring for cats, dogs, and the occasional parrot or two!